Saginaw Chippewa Academy LMC

NF          299 ROW          10158
Bowe, Anne          The secret name of Ra /

W9-BVC-180

WITHDRAWN

SAGINAW CHIPPEWA ACADEMY
LIBRARY MEDIA CENTER
MT. PLEASANT, MI 48858

Series Editor: Rosalind Kerven

© 1996 Rigby Education
Published by Rigby Interactive Library,
an imprint of Rigby Education,
division of Reed Elsevier, Inc.
500 Coventry Lane,
Crystal Lake, IL 60014

All rights reserved. No part of this publication may be reproduced or
transmitted in any form or by any means, electronic or mechanical, including
photocopying, recording, taping, or any information storage and retrieval system,
without permission in writing from the publisher.

Printed in Hong Kong

00 99 98 97 96
10 9 8 7 6 5 4 3 2 1

*Library of Congress Cataloging-in-Publication Data*

Rowe, Anne, 1935–.
     The secret name of Ra / retold by Anne Rowe;
    illustrated by Donald Harley.
       p.  cm. — (Myths and legends)
     Summary: Isis, the goddess of the dead, tricks Ra, the god of
  creation, into revealing his secret name so that she and her husband
Osiris can become rulers of the earth.
    ISBN 1-57572-016-7 (library)
    1. Ra (Egyptian deity)—Juvenile literature. 2. Isis (Egyptian
deity)—Juvenile literature. [1. Ra (Egyptian deity) 2. Isis
(Egyptian deity) 3. Mythology, Egyptian.] I. Harley, Donald, ill.
II. Title. III. Series: Myths and legends (Crystal Lake, Ill.)
BL2450.R2R68   1996
   299'.31—dc20                 95-38244

*Acknowledgments*
Title page, border, and map, pp. 2–3: Dave Bowyer;
photograph, p. 3: Werner Forman Archive

# The Secret
# Name of Ra

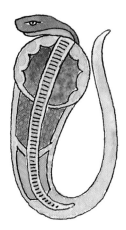

Retold by Anne Rowe
Illustrated by Donald Harley
Series Editor: Rosalind Kerven

# About the Ancient Egyptians

The Egyptian civilization is more than 5,000 years old.
The Ancient Egyptians were among the first
people to settle in one place and grow crops.
They lived around the Nile River, which flooded
every year bringing fertile soil.
They were ruled by very powerful kings called
pharaohs.
They invented picture writing called hieroglyphics.
We know from their writing that they believed
in many gods.

Map of Egypt

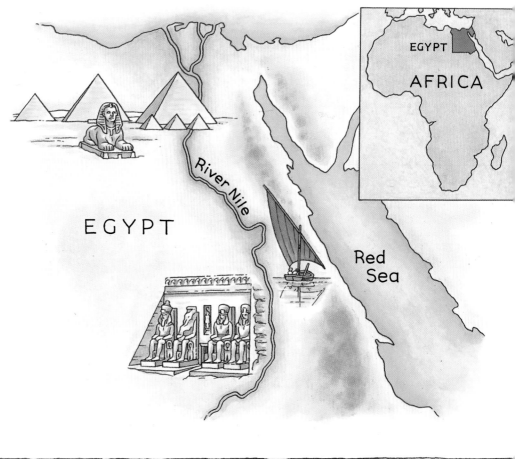

# Some Egyptian Gods

◀ Ra was the sun god, the king of the gods and the father of humankind.
He traveled across the sky every day.
People believed that his spirit lived in every pharaoh who ruled after him.

Osiris was the ruler of the Land of the Dead.
He built the first temples and designed the first statues.
He taught people how to make bread and wine. ▶

Isis was the mother goddess and a great enchantress.
She gave life, cured the sick, and could bring people back from death.
She taught people how to weave
◀ and how to grind corn.

When the tomb of the pharaoh, Tutankhamun, was opened, this gold mummy case showed the cobra on his headdress.
This story tells us why pharaohs wore the cobra. ▶

**R**a was the God of All Creation.
When he whispered the name of a living thing,
it sprang into life!
He named the creatures of the land, sea, and air,
and they came to life.
Last of all, he spoke the names of man and woman.

4

Ra himself had many names.
He was called the Dawn Beetle, the Sun God,
and the Eye of Heaven.
But he had one secret name.
It was so secret that he never said it out loud—
So secret that he never even thought it.
It was this secret name that gave Ra power over
all things and made him king of all the gods.

When Ra had made all the things on Earth,
he turned himself into the shape of a man.
He became Pharaoh.
He ruled over the Earth for a thousand years.

6

As time passed, Ra grew old and feeble.
Another god watched Ra grow old.
His name was Osiris.
He was the ruler of the Land of the Dead.
Osiris longed to rule over the Earth in Ra's place.

Osiris went to speak with his wife, Isis.
"I want to rule the Earth," said Osiris.
"How can I get rid of Ra and seize his power?"

Isis was a very powerful magician.
Surely there was something she could do
to help her husband.
She thought and thought.

"I must find a way to trick Ra into telling me
his secret name," said Isis.
"Each day he travels across his kingdom
from east to west.
I'll follow him and spy on him."
And so she hid herself, and watched and waited.

10

This daily journey was hard for someone as old as Ra.
When he stopped to rest, he took a drink
of the special water of life that he carried.
From her hiding place, Isis noticed how Ra's feeble
hand shook as he held the cup.
She saw how he trembled as he drank
the special water.
She saw him spill some of it.

Each day Ra stopped at the same place, and each day
he spilled some of the water of life.
This gave Isis an idea.
When Ra had left his resting place, Isis scooped up
the earth where he had spilled the water.
She moulded and pressed the damp earth
into the form of a snake.
She shaped a hood about its head, just like the crown
that Ra wore, to show that it was a royal beast.
Isis filled the lifeless snake with strong slow poison.
She put it where Ra would see it.

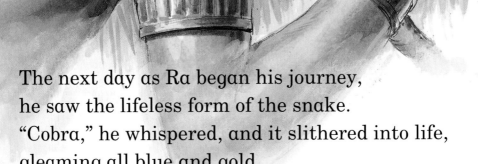

The next day as Ra began his journey,
he saw the lifeless form of the snake.
"Cobra," he whispered, and it slithered into life,
gleaming all blue and gold.

14

But when the snake saw Ra it reared up in fear.
It struck, biting Ra on the foot.
Ra screamed so loudly that the gods came rushing
to his side to see what had happened.
"I have been bitten by a snake that I did not make,"
said Ra.
"Someone is trying to kill me."
As Ra dropped to the ground in agony,
darkness fell over all the land.

The gods carried Ra to his palace.
He lay moaning with pain and fever.
All the while, the poison spread.
No one seemed to know what to do.

16

Isis waited.
The poison was slow but Ra, king of the gods,
did not die.
The poison was not strong enough to kill.
Isis wanted him to live, but she wanted him weak
and in her power.

17

Then Isis went to Ra and knelt beside him.
"I can cure you," she said.
"I will use all my powers, but I cannot show
my magic to others."
Ra ordered everyone to leave.
"Ra!" said Isis. "For my magic to work,
I must say all your names in my spell.

18

Tell me all your many names."
Ra said, "I am called the Dawn Beetle,
and I am called the Sun God,
and sometimes I am called the Eye of Heaven."
And he told her his many names.
But he did not tell her the name
that he dare not speak.

Isis built a fire and placed sweet smelling herbs
and incense upon it.
As the smoke drifted upwards, she began to chant.
She mixed a special potion as she sang.

20

Isis went on chanting but Ra's fever became worse.
"I must know your secret name," she insisted.
"Only that name is powerful enough
to fight off death."

The pain gripped Ra again.
"Come close," he whispered,
and he placed his hand on Isis' forehead.
"I cannot say my secret name out loud,
but I will think its shape into your mind."
And Isis saw in her mind his secret name—
**Amun**, the Hidden One.

As Isis began to chant again, she kept the secret
name, **Amun**, in her mind.
Isis gave her potion to Ra.
He sipped it and the fever began to fade.
The light returned.
Ra was cured,
but he knew that his power had left him.

Ra left the Earth to rule the sky.
Osiris and Isis became the new rulers.
They did not forget Ra, who had made all things.
Osiris built a temple and commanded all his people
to worship **Amun** Ra.